SLOTH

Coloring Book For Kids

This Book Belongs To

____

Color Test Page

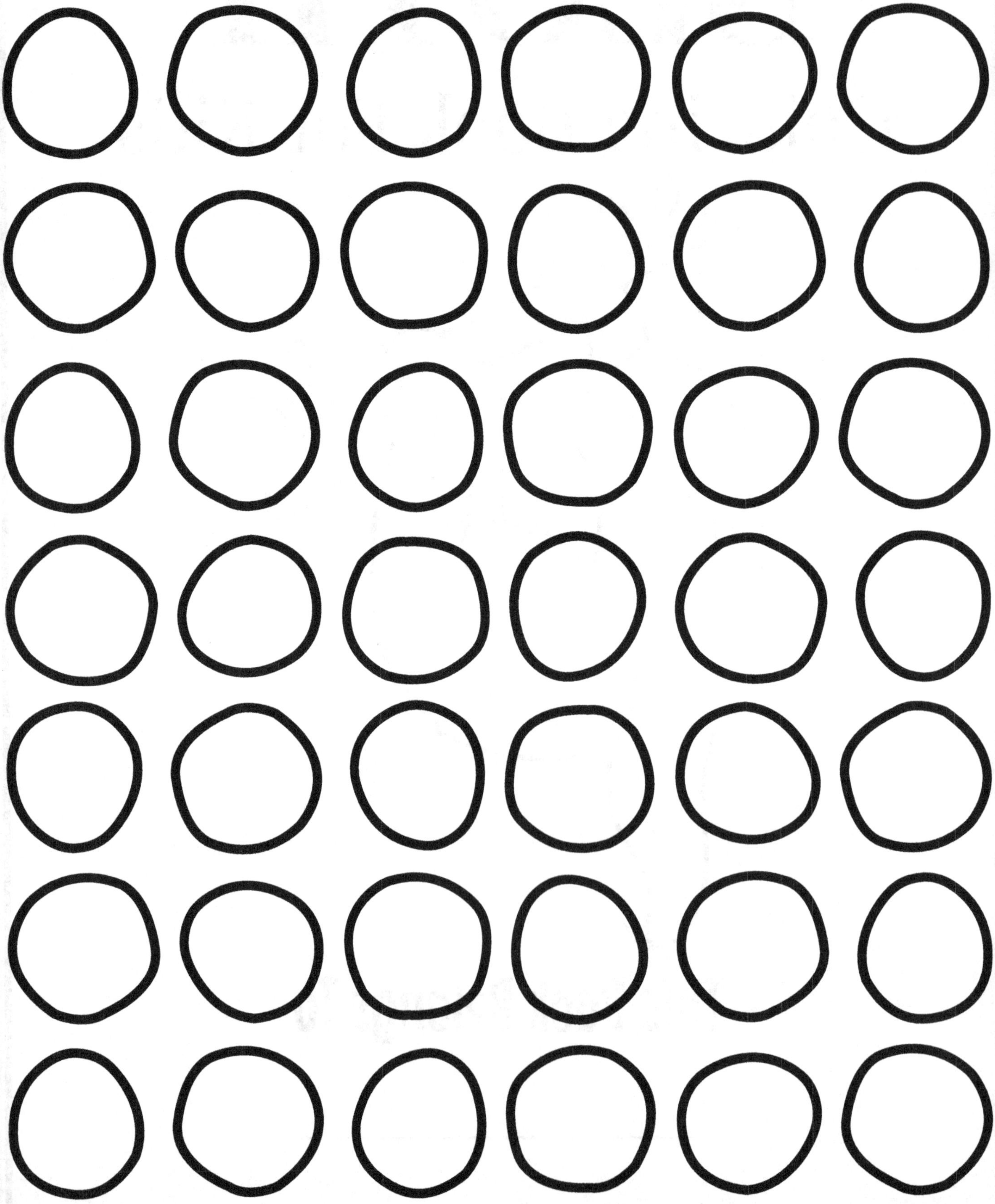

I ♥ YOU
mom

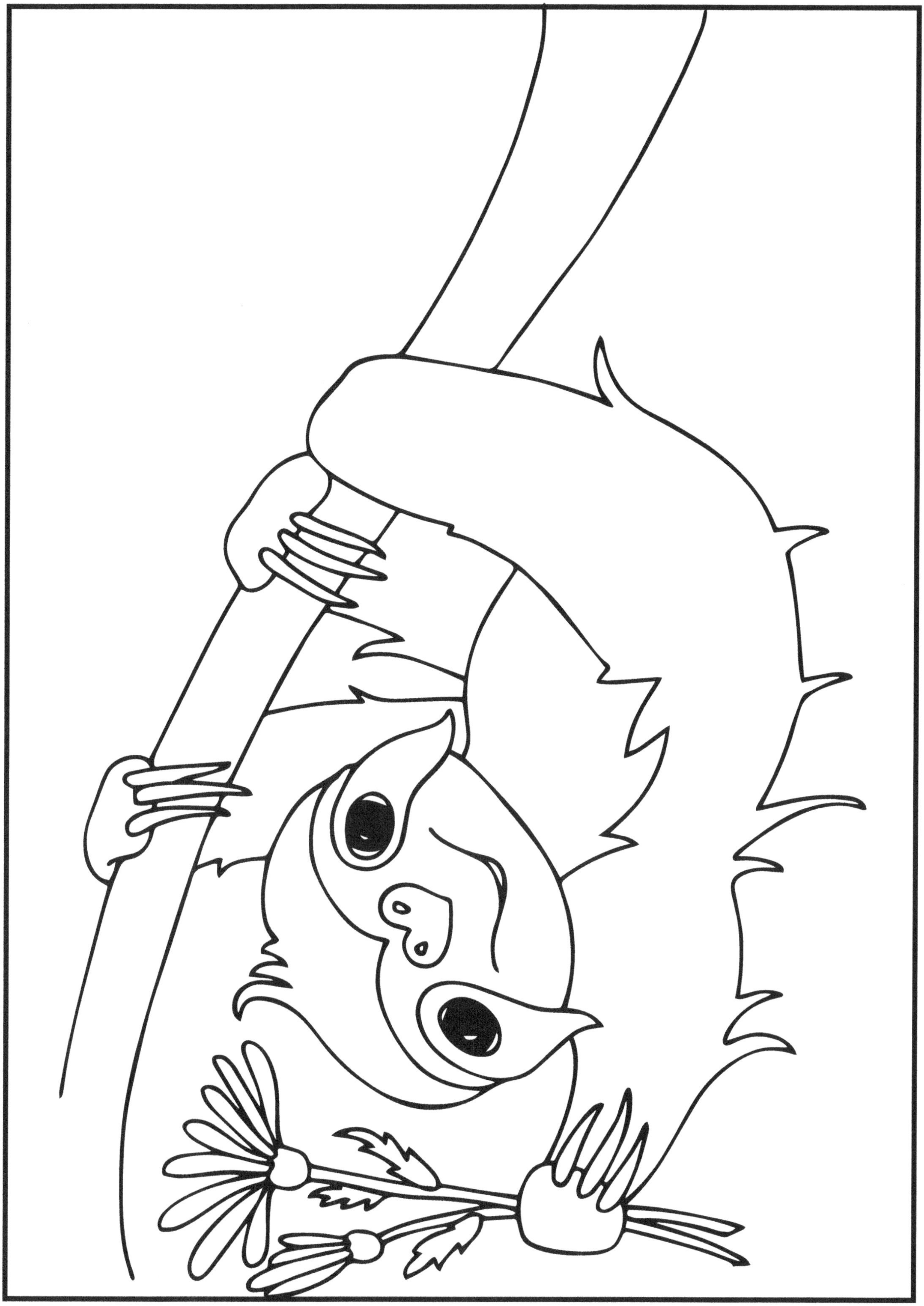

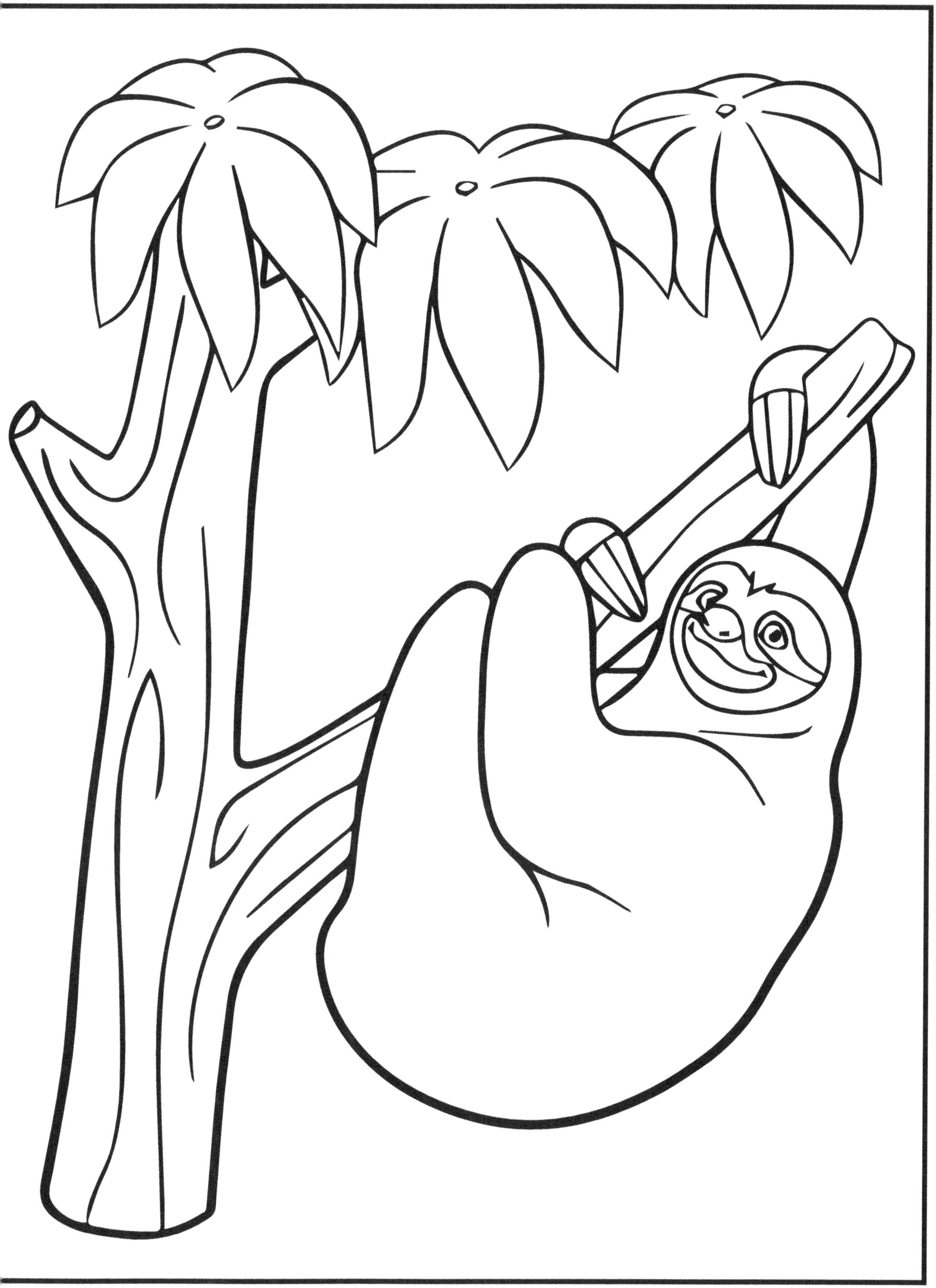

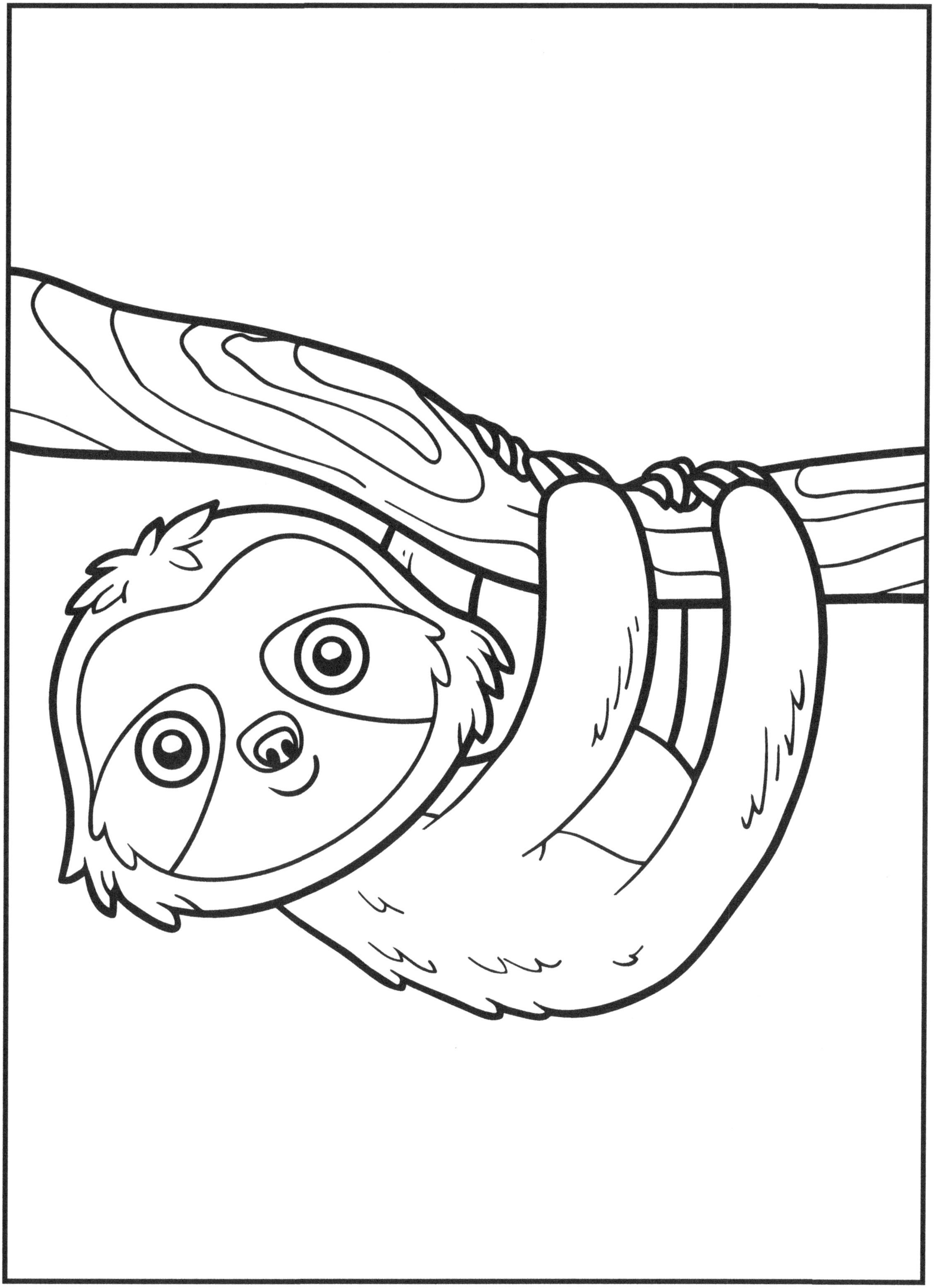

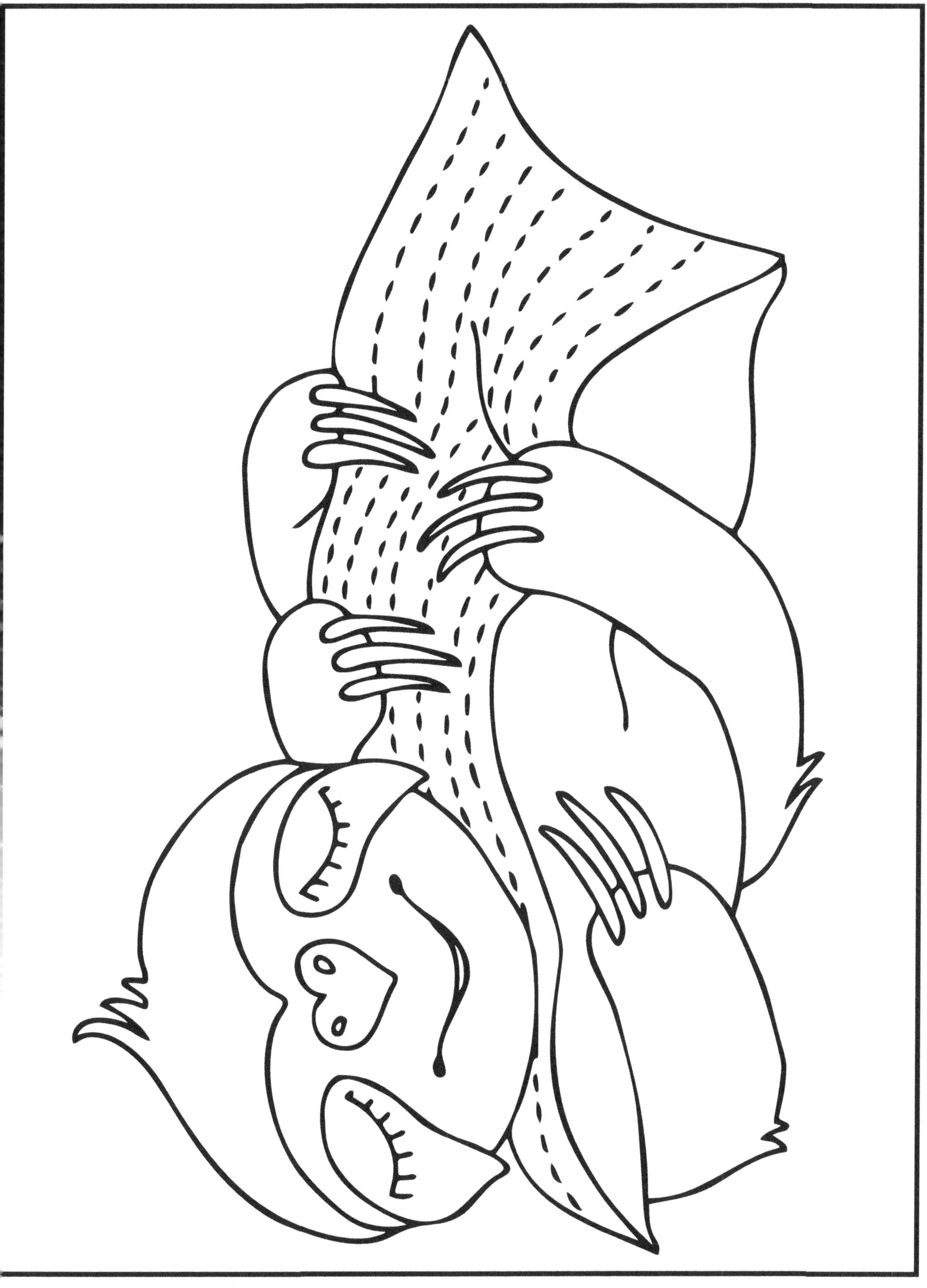

SUPER
HERO

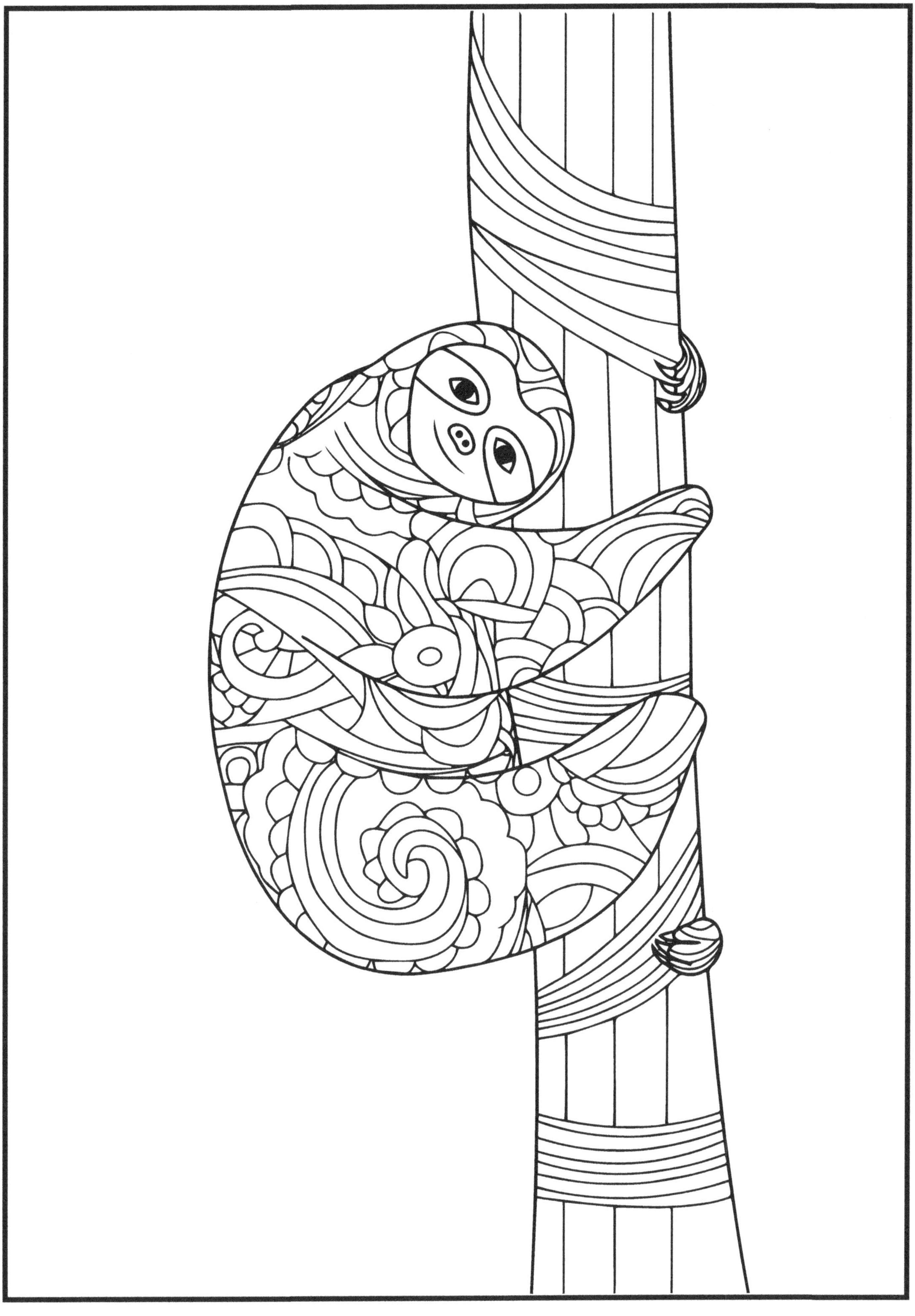

Made in the USA
Monee, IL
07 December 2023

48532269R00057